MEDIUM HIGH

Treasures for Solo Singers

10 Exceptional Vocal Solos for Recitals, Concerts, and Contests

COMPILED AND EDITED BY KATIE O'CONNOR-BALLANTYNE

Access the audio online as well as on the Accompaniment CD.

Alfred
Alfred Music
P.O. Box 10003
Van Nuys, CA 91410-0003
alfred.com

MEDIUM HIGH
Book & Online Audio (48587) ISBN-10: 1-4706-4325-1 ISBN-13: 978-1-4706-4325-6
Book (48588) ISBN-10: 1-4706-4326-X ISBN-13: 978-1-4706-4326-3
Online Audio (48589)
Enhanced CD (48590)

MEDIUM LOW
Book & Online Audio (48583) ISBN-10: 1-4706-4323-5 ISBN-13: 978-1-4706-4323-2
Book (48584) ISBN-10: 1-4706-4324-3 ISBN-13: 978-1-4706-4324-9
Online Audio (48585)
Enhanced CD (48586)

Cover Art: Vincent van Gogh (Dutch, 1853-1890).
Blühender Obstgarten, circa 1880-1890
Oil on canvas; 72 x 58 cm.
Private collection

About the artist: During his brief career, Vincent van Gogh completed several hundred paintings as well as numerous drawings and sketches. He suffered severe bouts of depression throughout his life, and created his most important works in the four years prior to his death. Although van Gogh is often considered an Impressionist painter, he had no connection to the French Impressionists, and his work remains highly individualistic in style.

1. AND THIS SHALL BE FOR MUSIC

Words by
ROBERT LOUIS STEVENSON (1850-1894)

Music and additional Words by
VICTOR C. JOHNSON

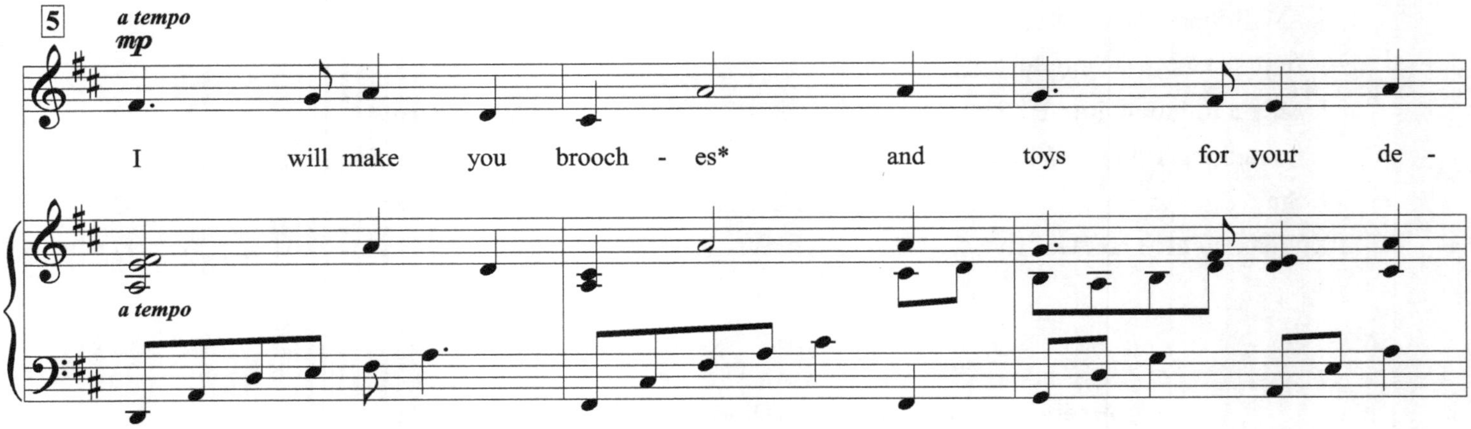

* Brooches (*broh-chehz*) - pieces of jewelry, usually fastened to clothing with a hinged pin and catch.

11
13
cresc.
star - shine at night. I will make a pal - ace
cresc.
15
mf
mp
fit for you and me, of green days in
mf
mp
18
mf
for - ests and blue days at sea. And
mf
22
this shall be for mu - sic when no one else is near, the

26
fine song for sing - ing, the rare song to hear! That
30
on - ly I re - mem - ber, that on - ly you ad - mire, of the
f
34
broad road that stretch - es and the road - side
mp
rit.
37
a tempo
fire.
39
gently moving
mf
I will make a crown for you of

41
ros - es, pure and white. And I will sing my
44
f
mp
rit.
f
song to you be - neath the glow of moon - light. And
f
mp
rit.
f
48
a tempo
this shall be for mu - sic when no one else is
a tempo
51
near, the fine song for sing - ing, the rare song to

55
56
mf
hear! That on - ly I re - mem - ber, that on - ly you ad -
59
f
mire, of the broad road that stretch - es,
62
mf
rit.
a tempo
mp
and the road - side fire. And
66
slowing to the end
p
this shall be for mu - sic.

2. BEYOND

Words by
JOHN PARKER

Music by
VICKI TUCKER COURTNEY

11
mf
13
place for you and me. Be - yond the mo-ments fond and
mf
14
ten - der, be - yond the days that used to be, be -
17
yond the min-utes we re - mem - ber, there is a time for you and
20
f
21
me. A - bove the blu - est sky, be -
f

23
yond the deep - est sea, be - yond the far - thest far, for-ev-er
27
poco rit.
mf
we will be, we will be! Be-
poco rit.
31
a tempo
fore the chill-y nights of win - ter, and af - ter fad-ing au - tumn
a tempo
mf
34
leaves, be - yond the fleet-ing hour of sum - mer, there is a

37
f
39
mem - ’ry of you and me. A - bove the blu - est sky, be -
f
41
yond the deep - est sea, be - yond the far - thest far, for-ev-er
45
mf
we will be, we will be, we will
decresc.
mf
49
rit.
mp
p
be, we will be!
rit.
mp
decresc.
p

3. COUNT THE STARS

Words and Music by
ANDY BECK

Expressively, with motion (♩ = ca. 104)

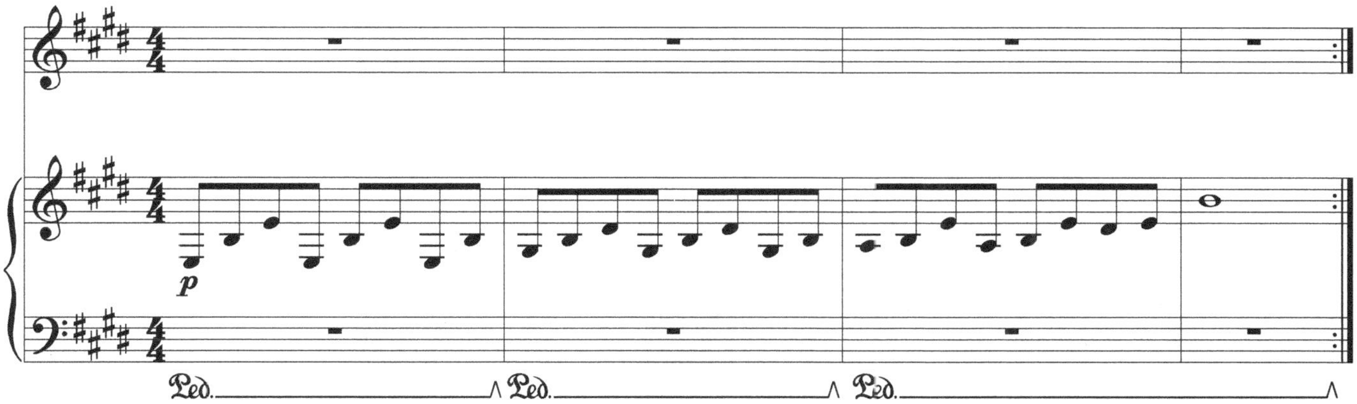

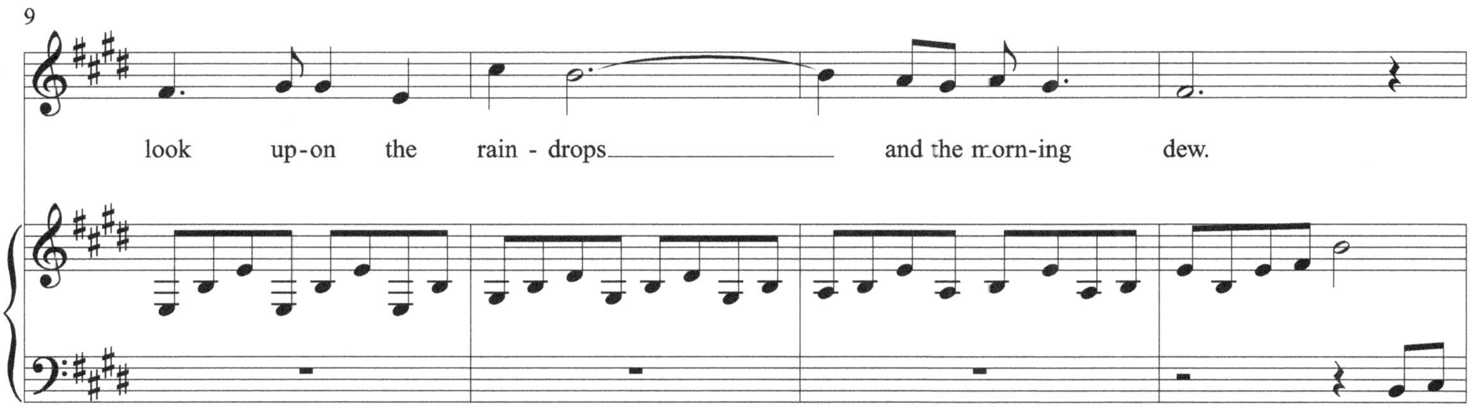

LATIN PRONUNCIATION:
Reh-kwee-ehm eh-tehr-nam daw-nah eh-ees, Daw-mee-neh: eht looks pehr-peh-too-ah loo-cheh-aht eh-ees.

13
cresc.
I will search the moon - beams, I'll ex - plore the ris - ing
cresc.
pedal harmonically
16
mp
decresc.
p
sun. And when the eve - ning comes, I'll count the stars,
mp
decresc.
p
20
cresc.
p
I'll count the stars.
cresc.
p
24
cresc.
cresc.

28
mp
Re - qui-em, re - qui-em ae - ter - nam
mp
32
cresc.
do - na e - is, Do - mi - ne: et lux per -
cresc.
36
mf
pe - tu - a, et lux per - pe - tu - a
mf
39
lu - ce - at e - is, lu - ce - at

43
mp rit. e decresc.
pp
e - is, lu - ce - at e - is.
mp rit. e decresc.
pp
47
a tempo
a tempo
p
Ped.
Ped.
Ped.
51
mp
I will count the stars for you. I will
mp
sim.
55
climb the high - est moun - tain, cross the o - cean, too.

59
cresc.
mf
I will watch the snow fall, I will lis - ten to the wind. And when the
pedal harmonically
63
decresc.
mp
eve - ning comes, I'll count the stars,
67
I'll count the stars,
71
rit. to end
p
decresc.
pp
I'll count the stars.
8va

4. GIFTS

Words by
SARA TEASDALE (1884-1933)

Music and additional Words by
VICTOR C. JOHNSON

13
a tempo
gave my first love laugh-ter, I gave my sec-ond tears, I
a tempo
mp
17
gave my third love si - lence through - out all the years.
21
mf
These are the gifts of love, so pre-cious_ and rare;
mf
25
full of ra - diant beau - ty, so bright and fair.

29
These are the gifts of love, that will nev - er___ de -
32
part; sa - cred, cher - ished mem - o - ries that
36
mp rit. a tempo
I hold___ in my heart.
mp rit. a tempo
40
mf con moto
My first love gave me sing - ing, my sec - ond eyes to
mf con moto

43
see.
But oh, it was my third love who
46
cresc.
gave my soul to me.
molto rit.
48
a tempo
f
These are the
49
gifts of love, so pre-cious and rare;
full of ra - diant
53
beau - ty, so bright and fair.

56
These are the gifts of love, that will nev-er de-part;
60
sa-cred, cher-ished mem-o-ries that I hold
64
mf
rit.
a tempo
in my heart.
67
mp
These are the gifts of
68
love.
rit. e decresc.
These are the gifts of love.
p

5. I WILL SING YOU THE STARS

Words and Music by
MARK BURROWS

Expressively, shimmering (♩ = ca. 92)

15
17
cresc.
run. You will fall, you will rise, you will
cresc.
19
mf
soar through the skies. Your new day has just be -
mf
23
mysterioso
mp
25
gun. And when dark - ness clos - es a - round you,
decresc.
mp
28
warmly
cresc.
I will send my love to sur - round you.
cresc.

33
mf
I will sing you the stars.
mf
37
Lift up your eyes wher - ev - er you are. You are
41
decresc.
not a - lone, love will call you home.
decresc.
45
poco rit.
a tempo
mp
I will sing you the stars.
poco rit.
a tempo
mp

49
54
mp
55
There are moun - tains you must climb.
58
There are path - ways you must tread.
You will
63
cresc.
give, you will grow, hold-ing on, let - ting go. A new jour - ney
mf

68
lies a - head.
mysterioso
mp
71
When you're lost and
decresc.
mp
72
doubt builds in - side you,
warmly
cresc.
I will send my
cresc.
76
love there to guide you.
79
f
I will
f
80
sing you the stars.
Lift up your eyes, wher -

85
87
ev - er you are. You are not a - lone, love will
89
decresc.
rit.
call you home. I will sing you the
decresc.
rit.
94
Slightly slower (♩ = ca. 84)
mp
decresc.
stars. I will sing you the stars.
mp
decresc.
99
rit. to end
p
I will sing you the stars, the stars.
8va
rit. to end
p

6. IN THE DARK OF MIDNIGHT

Words and Music by
ANDY BECK

13
thoughts are turned to you, my love, once more.
17
19
mp
Whis - pers on the wa - ter,
21
voic - es on the sea, though un - seen, they haunt and sum - mon
25
me.
mf
27
And they're call - ing me,
call - ing me
cresc.
mf

29
home.
And they're tell-ing me
not to
33
rit. e decresc.
35
a tempo
roam.
mp
37
poco rit.
a tempo
sim.
41
43
mp
In the dark of mid - night,

45
gaz - ing at the sky, there's a long - ing I can - not de -
49
ny.
53
mp
Moon, my on - ly com - fort; stars, my on - ly guide.
57
Con - jur - ing e - mo - tions from in - side. And they're
mf
cresc.

61
call-ing me,
call-ing me
home.
And they're
mf
65
rit. e decresc.
tell-ing me
not
to
roam.
rit. e decresc.
mp
69
a tempo
poco rit.
a tempo
At
mid - night.
a tempo
poco rit.
a tempo
74
rit. e decresc.
slowly
p
At
mid - night.
Mid - night.
rit. e decresc.
slowly
p
Ped.

7. MAY A RAINBOW RUN BESIDE YOU

Words from
Traditional Irish Blessings

Music by
MARK BURROWS

15
17
home.
May good and faith - ful friends be
20
mf
yours wher - ev - er you may roam.
May a
25
rain - bow run be - side you in a sky that's
mf
30
33
al - ways blue,
and may hap - pi - ness fill your

35
heart each day, and bless you your whole life
39
mf
through.
May
43
peace and plen - ty bless your world with
47
joy that long en - dures.
May

51
all life's pass - ing sea - sons bring the best to
56
you and yours!
f
59
May a rain - bow run be -
f
61
side you in a sky that's al - ways
65
67
blue, and may hap - pi - ness fill your

69
decresc.
heart each day, and bless you your whole life
decresc.
73
mf
75
through. And may hap - pi - ness fill your
mf
77
rit.
Slowly, freely
mp
heart each day, and bless you your
rit.
decresc.
mp
82
decresc.
whole life through.
8va
decresc.
p

8. SOMETHING TOLD THE WILD GEESE

Words by
RACHEL FIELD (1894-1942)

Music and additional Words by
ANDY BECK

13 A bit faster, delicately (♩ = ca. 84)
11
poco accel.
"snow." Leaves were green and stir - ring,
poco accel.
14
ber - ries, lus - ter - glossed, but be - neath warm
17
cresc.
feath - ers, some - thing cau - tioned "frost."
cresc.
20
f
So

23
fly, bird, fly. Win - ter's on the
f
26
wing. Good - bye, good - bye. Come a-gain next
30
decresc.
poco rit.
mf
32
a tempo
spring. All the sag-ging or - chards,
decresc.
poco rit.
a tempo
mf
33
steamed with am - ber spice, but each wild bird

36
stiff - ened at re-mem-bered ice.
39
40
Some-thing told the wild geese it was time to
42
fly. Sum - mer in their mem - 'ry,
45
win - ter in their cry.
f
So
cresc.

48
fly, bird, fly. Win-ter's on the
f
51
wing. Good - bye, good - bye. Come a-gain next
55
decresc.
rit.
mp
57 Tempo I (♩ = ca. 80)
spring. Some-thing told the wild geese it was time to
decresc.
rit.
mp
59
rit. e decresc.
Slowly, freely
p
go. Some-thing whis-pered "snow."
rit. e decresc.
p
Ped.

9. STAY

Words based on a poem by **MARGUERITE WIELE**
Adapted by **HERB FROMBACH**

Music by
VICKI TUCKER COURTNEY

13
stay, stay one more
17
mf
day. A
21
rose - bud, roy - al red, its thorns proud - ly guard - ing,
mf
25
breath - ing sub - tle, sweet - est per - fume. Oh,

29
stay, stay one more
33
35
day. A friend is like these, bring - ing
37
cresc.
joy to my heart, breath-ing love, life's own per -
cresc.
41
f
43
fume. Oh, stay, my friend.
f

45
rit. e decresc.
Stay one more day, one more
rit. e decresc.
49
a tempo
day.
mp
a tempo
53
mp
55
A li - lac, lav - en - der, an -
57
nounc - ing the spring - time, breath - ing sub - tle,

61
fra - grant per - fume. Oh, stay,
66
stay one more day. Stay one
70
rit.
decresc.
more day.
rit.
decresc.
p

10. WHAT DO THE STARS DO?

Words by
CHRISTINA ROSSETTI (1830-1894)

Music and additional Words by
VICTOR C. JOHNSON

13
What do the stars do up in the sky,
17
high - er than the wind can blow, or the clouds can fly?
21
mf
What do the stars do?
mp
What do the
mf
mp
24
poco rit.
a tempo
stars do?
poco rit.
a tempo

27
mf
Each star in its own glo - ry
mf
29
cir - cles, cir - cles still;
as it was lit to
32
f
shine and set
and do its mak - er's will,
f
35
mf
and do its mak - er's will.
rit.
8va
mf
rit.

38
a tempo
mp
What do the stars do up in the
a tempo
mp
41
sky, high - er than the wind can blow, or the clouds can
45
46
mf
fly? What do the stars do as they
mf
48
f
8
mf
glis - ten up a - bove? They il - lu - mi -
f
mf

51
poco rit.
nate all the earth with joy, hope, peace, and
poco rit.
54
a tempo
56
mp
love. What do the
a tempo
mp
57
poco rit.
stars do What do the stars do
poco rit.
60
Slowly, freely
p
decresc.
pp
up in the sky?
p
decresc.
pp